Measure with Metric

THOMAS Y. CROWELL COMPANY • NEW YORK

Measure with Metric

BY FRANKLYN M. BRANLEY

Illustrated by Loretta Lustig

? cm

? liters

? cm

YOUNG MATH BOOKS

Edited by Dr. Max Beberman, Director of the Committee on School Mathematics Projects, University of Illinois

BIGGER AND SMALLER *by Robert Froman*

CIRCLES *by Mindel and Harry Sitomer*

COMPUTERS *by Jane Jonas Srivastava*

THE ELLIPSE *by Mannis Charosh*

ESTIMATION *by Charles F. Linn*

FRACTIONS ARE PARTS OF THINGS
by J. Richard Dennis

GRAPH GAMES *by Frédérique and Papy*

LINES, SEGMENTS, POLYGONS
by Mindel and Harry Sitomer

LONG, SHORT, HIGH, LOW, THIN, WIDE
by James T. Fey

MATHEMATICAL GAMES FOR ONE OR TWO
by Mannis Charosh

ODDS AND EVENS *by Thomas C. O'Brien*

PROBABILITY *by Charles F. Linn*

RIGHT ANGLES: PAPER-FOLDING GEOMETRY
by Jo Phillips

RUBBER BANDS, BASEBALLS AND DOUGHNUTS:
A BOOK ABOUT TOPOLOGY *by Robert Froman*

STRAIGHT LINES, PARALLEL LINES,
PERPENDICULAR LINES *by Mannis Charosh*

WEIGHING & BALANCING *by Jane Jonas Srivastava*

WHAT IS SYMMETRY? *by Mindel and Harry Sitomer*

Edited by Dorothy Bloomfield, Mathematics Specialist, Bank Street College of Education

AREA *by Jane Jonas Srivastava*

BUILDING TABLES ON TABLES:
A BOOK ABOUT MULTIPLICATION *by John V. Trivett*

A GAME OF FUNCTIONS *by Robert Froman*

LESS THAN NOTHING IS REALLY SOMETHING
by Robert Froman

MEASURE WITH METRIC *by Franklyn M. Branley*

NUMBER IDEAS THROUGH PICTURES
by Mannis Charosh

SHADOW GEOMETRY *by Daphne Harwood Trivett*

SPIRALS *by Mindel and Harry Sitomer*

STATISTICS *by Jane Jonas Srivastava*

VENN DIAGRAMS *by Robert Froman*

Library of Congress Cataloging in Publication Data.   Branley, Franklyn Mansfield, 1915- Measure with metric. SUMMARY: Introduces the principles of the metric system through simple experiments. 1. Metric system—Juv. lit. [1. Metric system. 2. Measuring] I. Lustig, Loretta, Illus.   II. Title.   QC92.5.B7   389'.152   74-4056   ISBN 0-690-00576-8   ISBN 0-690-00577-6 (lib. bdg.)

1   2   3   4   5   6   7   8   9   10

Measure with Metric

YOUNG MATH BOOKS

? liters

? cm

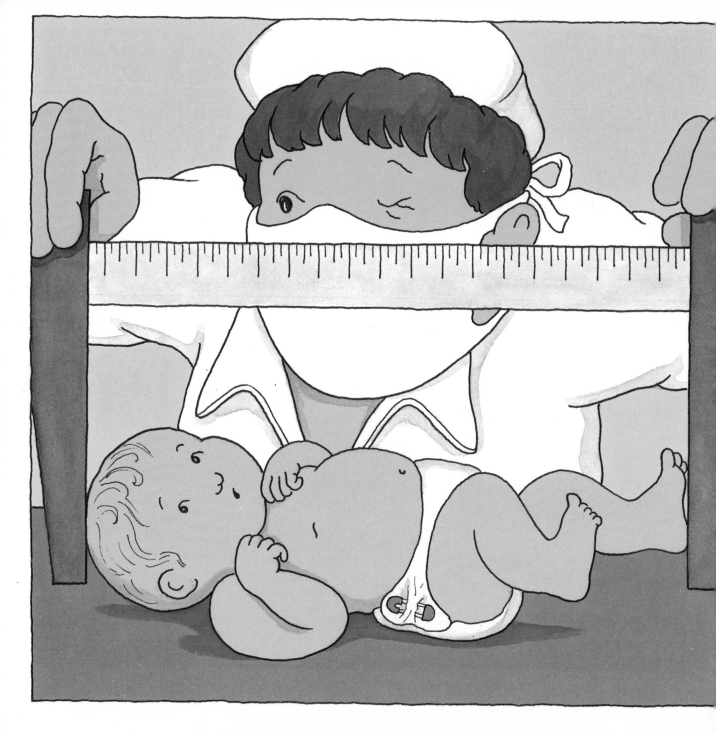

As soon as you were born, you were measured.

A nurse measured you from the top of your head to the bottoms of your heels. You might have been 19 inches long; maybe you were longer, or shorter.

The nurse weighed you, too. You might have weighed 8 pounds; maybe you weighed more, or maybe you weighed less.

lbs.

Suppose you had been born in Europe, or Asia, or South America, or Australia—almost anywhere in the world except the United States. Then your length would have been measured in CENTIMETERS, not inches. Your weight would have been measured in GRAMS, not pounds.

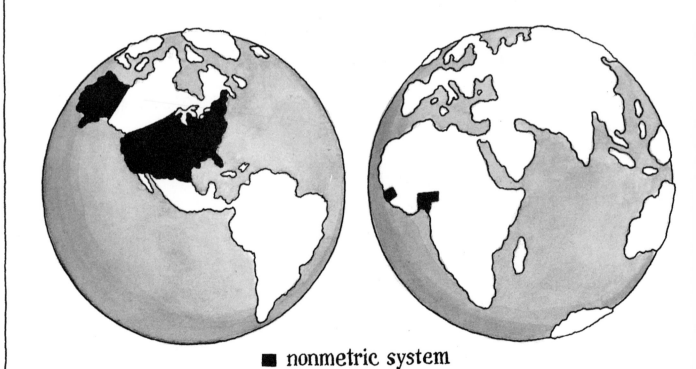

■ nonmetric system
□ metric system

Almost the whole world measures things in centimeters and grams. Centimeters and grams are part of the METRIC SYSTEM. Let's find out how people measure with metric.

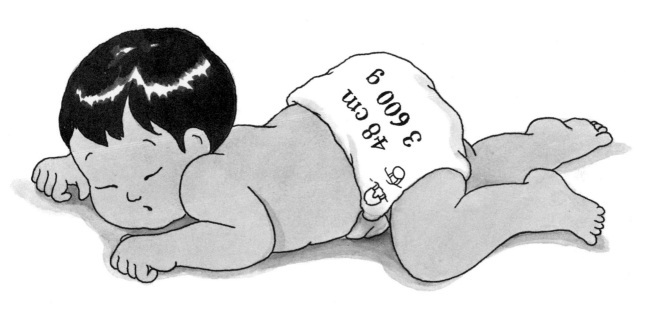

In the metric system, you might have been 48 centimeters long when you were born. You might have weighed 3 600 grams.

Today you're much longer. (We say you're much *taller* because now you don't lie down to be measured.) You are also much heavier.

Now you might be 140 centimeters tall, or maybe a bit taller or shorter. Let's find out how tall you really are in centimeters.

150 cm

145 cm

140 c

135

13

You'll need two narrow strips of cardboard. Sticks would be even better, if you have them. One should be short—just as long as the ruler shown here. The other stick should be longer. It should be at least ten times as long as the ruler in the drawing.

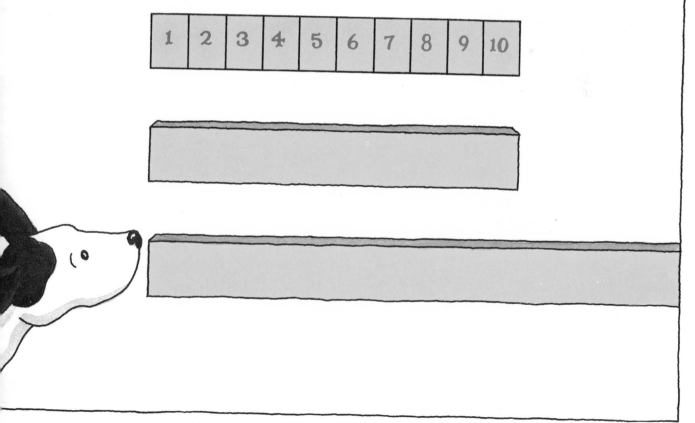

Lay the shorter piece of cardboard or stick just below the ruler on page 5. Copy each line and each number. You have made a ruler that is 10 centimeters long. Each small section is 1 centimeter.

Use your short ruler to make a longer one.

Lay the short ruler alongside the long stick. Start at one end and mark off ten lengths of the short ruler on the long stick. Make a long mark for each length. Make shorter marks for the

centimeters. Put the numbers 10, 20, 30, and so on, at the end of each long mark. Count the number of centimeters—all the long and short marks— that you have drawn. There are one hundred of them.

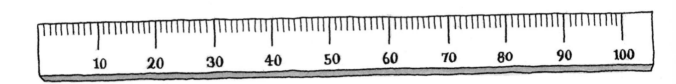

The long ruler is 100 centimeters long. It is called a METER RULER, or METER STICK. In 1 meter there are 100 centimeters. "Centi-" means "hundred." You already know there are 100 cents in a dollar. "Cent" also comes from a word that means "hundred."

Now let's measure. Stand with your back against the wall. Balance a book on top of your head. Have someone make a light pencil mark on the wall where the bottom edge of the book is.

Use your meter stick to find how far it is from the floor to the mark. Put one end of the stick on the floor. Make a small mark to show 1 meter. Now move the bottom of the stick to that mark. Count the number of centimeters to the mark that is even with the top of your head.

Maybe you'll find that you are just about 140 centimeters tall—100 centimeters (1 meter) and 40 centimeters more. Be sure to erase the marks on the wall.

You could say you are 140 centimeters tall, or you could say you are 1 meter and 40 centimeters tall.

How tall is your brother? How tall is your sister, your mother and your father, your cat or your dog? How high is a chair, a table, a doorknob?

How far is it across the room? How far is it from one end of your house to the other end? Use your meter stick to find out.

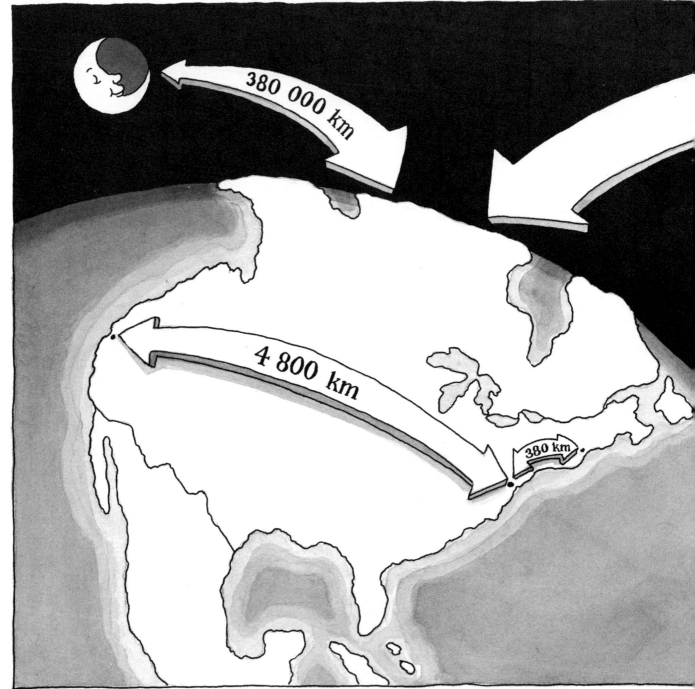

380 000 km

4 800 km

380 km

14

150 000 000 km

When long distances are measured, they are given in KILOMETERS. "Kilo-" means "thousand." A kilometer is 1 000 meters.

It's about 380 kilometers from New York to Boston; about 4 800 kilometers from New York to San Francisco; about 380 000 kilometers to the moon; about 150 000 000 kilometers to the sun.

6 g

150 g

7 000 g

1 500 g

5 000 g

2 000 g

50 g

2 000 000 g

When you were born, you might have
weighed 8 pounds, more or less. In the metric
system that would be 3 600 grams. In metric
we would say that your mass, which is your
weight at sea level, was 3 600 grams.

Now you weigh much more. You might weigh
40 000 grams, or 40 KILOGRAMS. From the
pictures you can see how much the dog weighs,
the cat, the elephant, and all the other animals.

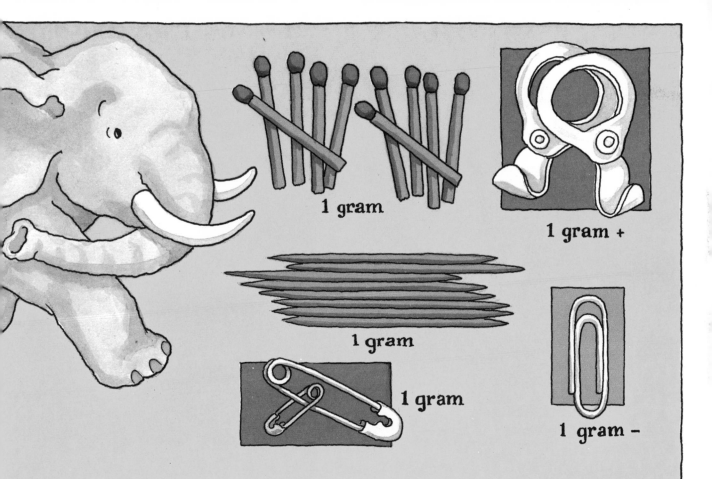

1 gram

1 gram +

1 gram

1 gram

1 gram –

A gram is not very much. We found that ten paper matches weigh 1 gram; two fliptops from soda cans weigh a little more than 1 gram; eight toothpicks weigh 1 gram. A paper clip like this one weighs just a little less than 1 gram. The two pins hooked together weigh 1 gram.

You can find the weight in grams of small, light things by making and using your own balance. You'll need an ordinary wooden ruler, 12 inches long. (You could use instead any piece of wood about 12 inches long that is thin and flat.) You will need a six-sided pencil, bottle or jar caps, some strong glue, a nickel, and some things that you can use for 1-gram weights. We used pairs of safety pins the same size as the ones in this picture.

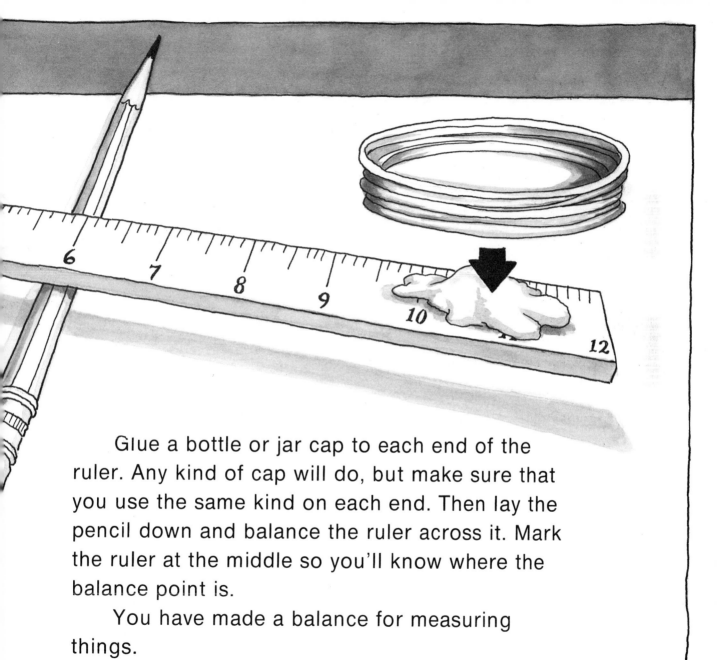

Glue a bottle or jar cap to each end of the ruler. Any kind of cap will do, but make sure that you use the same kind on each end. Then lay the pencil down and balance the ruler across it. Mark the ruler at the middle so you'll know where the balance point is.

You have made a balance for measuring things.

Put the nickel in one of the caps. Put 1-gram weights into the other cap until they balance the nickel. (If your fingers get in the way, use a pair of tweezers to lift things.)

As you're working, the ruler will tip to one side, and it may slide. Hold the ruler to the pencil by putting a finger at the balance point.

We needed five safety-pin pairs to balance our nickel. How many of your gram measures did it take? Since each pair of pins weighs 1 gram, and we used five pairs to balance one nickel, the nickel weighs about 5 grams.

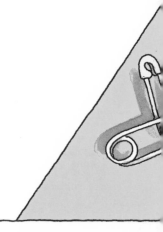

Let's find the weight of a dime. Put a dime on one side of your balance. You'll find that to make the two sides even, you must put in two of your special 1-gram weights and one smaller clip. You can say that the dime weighs a little more than 2 grams.

Find the weight in grams of other small things. Try a small nail, a thumbtack, a key, a small stone.

Some of them may weigh an even number of grams. You may need one, or two, or more of your special 1-gram safety-pin pairs. Or, maybe one safety-pin pair will be too much. Then you know the object weighs less than 1 gram.

Maybe you'll have to use the 1-gram pin pairs and also a smaller pin. Suppose the stone is balanced by three pin pairs and one smaller pin. You would know that the stone weighs a little more than 3 grams.

A gram is not very much. You weigh a lot of grams. A huge balance would be needed to find your weight. You can't use your little balance to weigh yourself in grams, but you can find your metric weight with a list here in this book.

Weigh yourself so that you know your weight in pounds. Find your weight, or the one close to it, on the list on the next page. Opposite it you will see your weight in grams.

If you weigh	then	*You weigh about*
40 pounds		18 250 grams
45		20 500
50		22 750
55		25 000
60		27 250
65		29 500
70		31 750
75		34 000
80		36 250
85		38 500
90		40 750

How many grams do you weigh?

Suppose you weigh 34 000 grams. That is 34 kilograms. Did you remember that "kilo-" means "thousand"?

Suppose you weigh 29 500 grams. That is 29 kilograms and 500 grams. In metric we write 29.5 kilograms and say, "twenty-nine point five kilograms" or "twenty-nine and a half kilograms."

You have measured the metric length of
rooms, and the metric height of a table, a chair, a
dog or cat. Also, you know the metric weights of
dimes and nickels, stones, paper clips, yourself.
Now, you can measure liquids using the metric
system.

In the metric system, pints, quarts, and
gallons are not used to measure milk, ice cream,
cider, or gasoline. Instead, LITERS are used.
("Liter" rhymes with "beater.")

You can make a box that will hold just about 1 liter. Follow the directions below. If you have any trouble, ask someone to help you.

Use your short ruler, the one that is 10 centimeters long. Make five squares of cardboard, each square 10 centimeters on a side. Put marks 1 centimeter apart on four of the squares; they should look like the ones in the picture.

Using tape, fasten the squares together to make a box. The marks should be on the inside of the box. Put a few long pieces of tape all around the box to make it stronger.

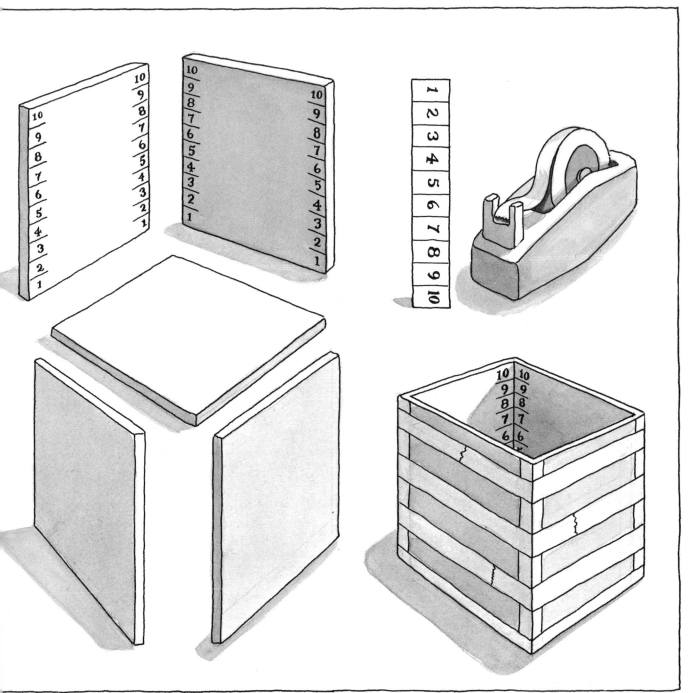

27

You have made a LITER BOX. The box is 10 centimeters long, 10 centimeters wide, and 10 centimeters high. When it is filled right to the top, it holds 1 liter. If it is filled to the "4" mark, it holds 4 DECILITERS. There are 10 deciliters in 1 liter. "Deci-" means "ten."

Let's use the box to measure a glass of water, a bottle of soda, and other quantities of liquids. (You had better do this in the sink in case your liter box should come apart.)

Put a plastic bag in the liter box so it will hold water. Push the bag to the edges of the box. (Make sure the bag is big enough to get into the corners.) Pour a glass of water into the plastic bag. What part of a liter is the glass of water?

Suppose that the water comes up to the "3" mark on your box. You would say that the glass of water is 3 deciliters.

How many deciliters is a bottle of soda? How many deciliters is a pint; a quart?

In the metric system you buy milk by the liter, or the half liter. You buy gasoline by the liter; a tankful would be about 80 liters. You use about 50 liters of water to take a bath.

How many liters did you drink yesterday? Add together the water, milk, orange juice, cocoa. You'll probably find that you drank about 2 liters—even more if you were especially thirsty.

Now you know how to measure with metric. That's the way almost everyone in the world measures things—all except people in the United States and a few very small countries. Someday people in the United States will measure with metric, too.

Start measuring with metric. Pretty soon everyone will.

ABOUT THE AUTHOR

Franklyn M. Branley, Astronomer Emeritus and former Chairman of The American Museum–Hayden Planetarium, has written many books, pamphlets, and articles on various aspects of science for young readers. He is the author of *Think Metric,* a book for older boys and girls about the metric system. MEASURE WITH METRIC is Dr. Branley's first book for the Young Math series.

Dr. Branley holds degrees from New York University, Columbia University, and the State University of New York College at New Paltz. He and his wife live in Woodcliff Lake, New Jersey, and spend their summers at Sag Harbor, New York.

ABOUT THE ILLUSTRATOR

Loretta Lustig was graduated from Pratt Institute and has worked as an art director for several advertising agencies. She has illustrated children's books on widely different subjects (her first book was about garbage!). Ms. Lustig enjoys reading odd things, making odd things, and collecting odd things, and she lives in Brooklyn, N.Y., which she has found to be the ideal place.